Making the Bed

Making the Bed

Poems by
Ruth Moose

Ruth Moose (signature)

MAIN STREET RAG PUBLISHING COMPANY
CHARLOTTE, NC

©Copyright 1995, 2004 by Ruth Moose
All rights reserved
Second Printing

Cover art and design by Talmadge Moose

Acknowledgments:

The poem "Homeless" was published in *Christian Century*
"Bloodroot" was published in *Embers*
"Work" appeared in *The Other Side*
"Yes" was published in *Sundog*
"Housecleaning" was published in *Crucible*
"Leaf Raking" appeared in *New Virginia Review*
"Findings" was purchased by *McCall's*
"Blackberry Wine" appeared in *Christian Century*
"Father, Son and Oranges" won First Prize at Augusta College

ISBN: 978-1-930907-43-0
ISBN: 1-930907-43-5

Originally published by Sandstone Publishing
Reprinted by

Pure Heart Press/
Main Street Rag Publishing Company
PO Box 690100
Charlotte, NC 28227-7001
www.MainStreetRag.com

CONTENTS

Original Knowledge
    The First Morning 11
    Original Knowledge 13
    Eve Looks Back 14
    Picking Cherries 15
    The Snake 17
    Children at Dusk 18
    Homeless.. 20
    Bloodroot 21
    Work.. 23

Yes
    Swan Lake 27
    828 Woodland Street.. 29
    Winter, During the War....................................... 31
    Stories 32
    Buttermilk... 35
    The Marriage of Waters 36
    Comfort 38
    Housecleaning.. 39
    Leaf Raking Poem 41
    Yes 43
    Dowry 44

Making the Bed
    Staying Over... 47
    Making the Bed 48
    Laundry... 49
    Another Name.. 50
    Marriage Portions 51
    Safe Houses 52
    Findings 54
    Tin Years 55

On Her Way to Meet Her Lover,
She Forgives Her Father 56
Father, Son and Oranges 59
Bagpipes 61
Dialogue: Mother to Son 63
Sunday in the Park with God and Sparrows ... 65

Sleep
    Penelope, After 69
    George Eliot: Letter to John Cross 70
    He Licked Wine From My Fingers 71
    River Bed 73
    Blackberry Wine 75
    Double Bed 76
    My Grandfathers Bed 77
    Afternoon of a Father-in-Law 78
    Crocheted 80
    Flannel Pajamas 81
    Sleep 82
    Single Bed 83

*To Talmadge
(Better never than late?)*

Original Knowledge

All knowledge is original knowledge

The First Morning

The first morning
Eve woke up
looked at the man beside her
and thought, "Who the hell is this?"
His snoring was the sound of animals.
He hadn't shaved in a week
and his touch was not one she'd choose
for herself. She moved
her bed elsewhere.
It wasn't as warm
but at least fresh smelling
like flowers . . . gardenias, honeysuckle,
jasmine, roses and more.
She had named the flowers . . . dahlia, zinnia,
hibiscus, hydrangea, nasturtium (try saying
that through your nose), portulaca
(a fun one she thought), phlox,
agapanthus he would never have
named in a million years.
She, herself, had started
with poppy, daisy, begonia
and rose
moved up to those.
Eve made naming the flowers
her chosen work. He had enough
and more with the animals. Even
then it was she who thought of
hippopotamus, rhinoceros, zebra
and armadillo. Adam was not
a word person. His taste ran
more to bear, fox, wolf, lion

and hawk. Deer was one
of hers he especially liked.
You can see why.
He's used it ever since
often times for her.
It was easy.
The question for her
was what next.

Original Knowledge
(A Confession of sorts)

In all that flowering and fruiting,
forbidden lushness, of course I knew.
No one had to write me a book.
He never believed I had a headache
and as I grew full as an apple,
rounding every curve, he thought
it might be the climate. How
could anyone remain innocent
around animals? They came
with the landscape,
first two, then
others after something I saw.
No one had to whisper anything.
I tell you all you had to do was look.
And I had plenty of time for that.
There was only trees, water,
stones and the sky for company.
Long ago I learned lavender makes
a better pillow than flax, but
you can sleep on anything
if your days are dull. We had seasons
of sleep. Even light closed its eyes
and a rounder One looked dimly down.

That started it.

Eve Looks Back

The God who married
Adam and Eve wasn't
her father though she'd been
warned by the worm
things would change.
She thought better,
never worse. Optimist
she'd always been,
gave it a try; a spin
of a year and by then
there was too much to move,
nowhere to go. Home to Mom?
A laugh. Besides it rained
daily in that thick garden.
Here at least she had a roof.
Thatched by light, it kept
wind out, though shadowed
by anything that climbed and
that was a lot; animals with tails,
those not, like the worm,
lavender in his leaving.

No bureau to undo what she'd done,
no judge to say what went
to whom. He could have the children,
both boys, bronze and smart
mouthed. She knew their kind.

She wanted what
she'd never had.
God knows the place,
the price.

Picking Cherries

Joy hangs for the reaching.
I stretch until I am beyond
ladder and body and breath.

You tilt in the tree opposite,
climbing as I climb. We climb
past finger pointing scarecrows,
tin pans and a dead blackbird
to show God means business.

Time has carried us here
above the ground.
Time, that tired man
on a wooden horse,
not the white stallion
I dreamed. You stole me
from a father who put his princess
on a high horse with silver
stirrups. We streamed away
in a blue Plymouth of words,
bells clanking, "You fools,
you fools."

There were others in the tree
before us. Morning before late
afternoon, but I never say
who as I sit in my bark saddle
chanting can she bake a cherry pie,
charming, charming cherries
into my fingers. Mother never knew
you had the small heart of me
under apples on a hot Sunday.
Grass embossed your back
like wires, thick and deep.

It is in the tree we see
where we are and how far
we have to fall. We choose,
or someone else loosens
the rung. Someone
who leads us to think
a foothold is beneath
when it's not.

The Snake

Like a garter it lay
round, brown circle,
elastic, leather with white
underneath. Head the shape
of a diary lock. Rattle.
A key in my mind rattled.
I killed him first.
All the way home something
curled around my ankle
hissed its name.

Children at Dusk

I dreamed of caladiums,
those brown runes
planted beneath oaks.
A dozen bulbs
nestled in warm earth
a thousand Aprils ago.
I dreamed they bloomed
green and white in another place
where children played.
Bloomed red and silver
in that place where it stayed
dusk always and the tired, hysterical
screams of children happily
held off night.

Think of those sounds.
How they surprised even you
in their fierce strength
saying you would not come in.
That it wasn't night, not yet.
Not dark at all. Let you watch
the stars come out. Let you run
one more round of Hide and Seek
in the falling dew. Let you hide
and stay hidden until the dark
was gone and you were safe,
truly safe after all.
Your teeth glowed in a grin
hat scared your brother.
Your cool hands on his shoulder
made him shiver and your toes
in the sharp grass were colder
than the moon.

Stars bloomed
in a field just beyond
the tallest tree.
Below there were caladiums
bending in light, bowing
to a different darkness
but close as brothers
hiding and seeking,
teasing away
what they'd never say.

Homeless

I was five, wearing tight
braids, plaid bows in our small
towns largest department store.
Stairs going up, down
a thousand faces met, passed,
followed me. If no one claimed
me I was free between floors
and the ultimate earth.
Hanging by my name
no one knew Between the avenues
of dresses, the institutions
of suits, business of shoes,
crowd of hats and hands of gloves,
I could walk in the light of selling,
the merchandise of good times
until I came to the end of the stairs,
and stopped. Waiting to go on
listening for one word
from a voice I knew,
couldn't hide,
nor deny.

And my eyes
soon asking as those
in shelters
seek something no one can say
for them.

Bloodroot

How can I tell you about that winter?
Everything froze, even my chest.
Days were nights.
It always rained.
Snow slid off the roof in thunder.
The house had walls, no windows.
I slept with my head in a hole.
Nothing melted.
A pileated woodpecker attacked
the front yard pines, screaming.
He echoed my eyes.
There were beams in my heart,
roofing nails where we walked;
paths we made mornings
trying to find hope.
We lived with lumber towering
from floors. Lumber not for walls,
nor fireplace, except ends and limbs
wind laid at the door.
We went suited for sorrow, but some spark
flickered deep, small. Nothing sang
but debts doled out by bankers, plumbers,
trees of snow were sun and night;
nothing to take us toward anything warm.
I paced bare boards, called the moon.
Silver naked, shadow slim in its light,
I asked for warmth, answers to frozen soles.
Days I hung our knitted selves to air,
felt only bones and skin until our
cotton coats of mail covered all but face
and fingers, feet. Without them, I never felt
so bare. Homeless was only numbers away.
There was ice on the creek and willow leaves

tainted our coffee and tea.
Twigs wore coats of cold.
When we poured them in, they broke.
Like we felt. Like we looked.
We hid from everyone we knew.

Through rain, I cried a sky,
a lake undone. At my feet Bloodroot
unfolded a message
in snow.

Work

We need work.
Our hands ask for it.
Our minds beg direction,
answers to be classified.
Positions held before us
like treats, tidbits, tokens
to enter the rest of the world.

We make work
but it does not pay.
The fun with our fingers
is only amusement;
cat's cradles, magic tricks
that fumble and fail,
delight us least of all.

The rest of the rush
is not us. We want
to walk in step, carry briefcases
or ladders, be a bonus at year's end,
sign up for vacation earned,
not imposed, assigned.

Minds need meaning
to attach to days
like tickets
to a distant station
where the conductor waits,
lifts his cap,
and wipes his brow.
Even he has
work.

Yes

Swan Lake

With scissors that summer
we made a stage. Your porch
behind the swing, dressingrooms,
wings right and left, audience
between geraniums and fern.
Our fingers danced days
in pretense, nights
in the dream store.
We kissed pillows,
whispered what our names
would be. Yellowed pages
were all we had as daughters
of the dedicated mothers
as dedicated as their mothers,
who could not know evils
in the trading places, sacks
of black feathers. They guided
us to guard paste rubies
like real for the right one.
Those thieves! Unlocked our legs
smooth as water over stones.
There was no stopping
and damned, no way back.
We washed; our desires
caressed like first stockings
in heels that made us taller.
Those earrings pinched and marred,
and no one told us gold goes green.
In straps and snapping garters,
we buckled up for approval,
down for dares. Gone were
lets pretend lives.

We water-proofed our lips
in 48 shades for the waves
that were dark and warm and ours.
They knew our names, sang beneath
our feet. Thieves came back
disguised in charm, claimed us
at the end of an aisle
where we spun on our toes
wearing flowers, tiaras and pearls.

Princes whose kingdoms were straw.
We lived naked, blind and mute
until one day in the last looking
place, we found our wings,
put them on and flew.

The sky was the same and knew us.
Water had waited. We had only
forgotten the power
in owning
what had always been ours.

828 Woodland Street

Assignment: Design, draw and color to scale the redecoration of a room in your home. Student must do all work with no adult assistance.

Even the bed was borrowed.
Navy blue and not really a bed at all,
but an armless, backless sofa
with missing pillows. A neighbor,
who had more furniture than house,
and a daughter who entertained
on a newer couch, loaned us
the old sofa. It smelled of storage,
attic and something I could never
quite name. Its prickly cover
itched through three quilts. No wonder the
neighbor's daughter, whose name was Betsy
Jo, discarded it. Betsy Jo's name around
town was "Boxcar" because she once
"entertained" four boys in one. But that
was only rumor and certainly nothing her
mother should know. And it had nothing
to do with the sofa which was all there
was in my room except a desk and chair.

I didn't know Thoreau then, but I think
of him now when I measure that room
in my mind. One window, a small, square eye
wore lace curtains kept tight
top and bottom with a rusted rod.
What hung on the walls was hope,
thumbtacked, taped and overlapped
postcards of Paris, London, Rome,
the Grand Canyon, Black Hills, Painted
Desert, Redwood Forest and a hundred
places from a bird's eye view.
And mine at 828 Woodland Street

when I was thirteen and took Home Economics
under Mrs. Strindhaus, Home Project,
one half your semester grade, due Dec. 1.

Boxes and boxes, plus two trunks
owned that room of little light.
I bought fabric and paint…
the floor a deep sea green
like walking on water always cool.
Spread and pillows, I stitched
from blue polished cotton, orange poppies
and pink sweetpeas, curling tendrils
like waiting asps. In the desk,
a monogram diary lay written in code
too complicated even for Nancy Drew.
I was Heidi in her sweet loft,
Anne Frank wondering about the world
and workings of her own pale body. I
slept in girl curlers of wire and brush.
My glow-in-the-dark cross guaranteed
nothing evil could come.

This was 828 Woodland Street
with neither a tree nor woods
in sight. We had to climb ligustrum
shrubs for berry wars. I was forty
before I learned Woodland had been
the lumber company that cut
down all the trees. But this was
after the postcard places and I came
back to no house, but an apartment
building 3 stories tall and the whole
street windows of wall.

Beneath the last complex, buried
in earth or between some shoulders
of stone, there must be a blue glint
of postcards sea or sky. Surely
some shred of the girl who was me.

Winter, During the War

I wake in a room of wood whorls
counted to sleep in a bed vacated
by my mother and six aunts in turn
who left behind a wardrobe wearing
hats to the ceiling, bursting
with clothes I paraded, shoes loud
as drums. Ghosts of girls flash
the mirror freckled as fish
in a pool reflecting a garden
of croton flowers, petals
of dried perfume.

A slit of light slides under my door,
then silhouettes, voices from
the Dr. Christian Show. Will she
be all right? The china doorknob
is cold as an egg. I see Grandmother
kneeling on the red rug beside her bed.
In her flannel gown, she is an illustration
from my book of bedtime prayers.
The woodstove, banked for the night, grins
death. The disappearing doctor's car
slices dark trees and hills in half.
Mother rests in the large front room.
Blood that would have been my brother,
bedclothes that caught him, wait
a shoebox burial. War, my grandmother
says, is hard on women. She warms me
into her bed, yanks out the light.

Stories

I was five, brother three,
our story book was Bible
with Jesus on the front.
Lambs played behind him,
kids sat on his knee. Inside
we read of Baal and parents
who sacrificed children
to the firest fire. Mama,
who bought the book, said
a thousand times she wished
she hadn't, promised a thousand
times not to shove us in the furnace.
We studied the horrible heat
leaping larger than volcanoes.
In our bellowing nightmares
yawning furnaces of flames
swallowed good children and bad
feeding the king of sin.

That summer there were polio children.
Not us, but news in the papers, on radio.
We had fevers, dry throats, kept
from pooi and park. The front walk
our boundary. She read to us,
played Hearts, Crazy Eights, walked
ten blocks to bring new games,
balloons, scissors and glue,
things to keep us safe.

Lindberg baby stolen from his crib.
Even newsmen cried telling about
his cap and sweater, other remaining
things. She put hands over our ears,

said don't walk near bushes, get in cars,
take gum or candy or money from men.

There were magic bubbles
blown from a tube, pipe.
Stayed for hours, days, weeks,
forever soft if you didn't chew
pink ooze from the spout,
tasting like rocks and rain, foreign things.
We didn't tell her, waited
for news of our own dark flights
or forever pain.
Life was a magazine;
war, concentration camps.
No one we knew but their eyes
met ours in something larger
than all of us. She let neighbors,
who were strangers, share
our wailing nights when search lights
walked the street. It won't hurt,
she said. It's all right. Answers
comforted like blankets and syrup
for winter ills.

Mother met the world
in a linen suit, leather pumps,
felt hat, brave red feather.
She stood one foot behind, one ahead,
on a path no one dared go around.
Nothing stopped her
except our tall father.
What lies did he feed her? Promises
of thirty-six lost years; new rugs,
fanlight for the front door?
She always settled for less
than even the most that could
have been. One rose rather

than the arbor he swore he'd build.
Instead he made a hunting lodge,
furnished with skins, fireplace
for thawing ghosts. Our faces
hung on the rafters. Father,
whose biggest sport was conquests
and tales. Father, in the late,
gray morning, mother in her gown,
apron over for breakfast,
flowers she bought herself.
Father forgot, forgot, forgot. Except
the other house there was wine
and music, no time for anyone
but two.

It won't hurt, she told us. It's
all right, she said. No one told
her. I say it now. Pretty stories,
little lies we keep to the end.

Buttermilk

They knew the moon
and the moon knew them,
five females in various women forms
mooned the earth, giving their sweet
stream back in a song that said
"Alive, alive." Laughing, long-haired,
girls in nightgowns, their feet white as shells.
In summer crickets sang, distant dogs barked.
Winter they wore the warmth
from a wood fire toward the same
scene the moon saw.
The ritual of opening themselves
like an internal eye, a secret eye
to the earth that bore them.
Pretended they were going to tell the moon
goodnight.
White as biscuits, mounds of dough
that rose to the occasion. Soft dust
disturbed the chicken, though
the cats long ago claimed circles
under porch.
Earth was all around and ready
to receive even an ounce
of what it had given.

Daughters of Venus
outside in their own shells.
Earth's daughter, earth's mothers.

A long path led
to the half moon house
and in the dark, things
in the weeds moved, whispered.

The Marriage of Waters

1.
Sparrows in the rain barrel.
Unimportant death
flung against the waters,
dark and full of thunder.
Small, naked feet, outspread
and floating
as though they reach
for something pale
in captured clouds,
then fell, and falling
lost all air.

2.
By the backporch roof
where apples dried in curls
grandmother dropped peelings,
initials of who I'd marry.
Hers had been wrong. I promised
I wouldn't, but did, despite
her warnings and worries.
I feel her now, soft hands
on my shoulders as I sit
at grandfather's rolled oak desk.
A wicker lamp swings
above us like a lifetime. Shadows
cut behind the wardrobe where I wept
in Confederate gray, hot in wool
and mothballs until the relatives left.
Grandfather switched the radio
to Jesus Saves, cold biscuits,
fresh blackberry jelly and me.

3.
In feather pillows,
I dream of drowning.
An unknown sea flat and black
waits hollow bones, no boat,
no oars, or air to clutch.
The room is a robe around me;
husband, children, rain fills
the barrels of my pockets.

Comfort
(for M.)

What you mourn for
isn't what you think.
The name you call, shouting
back years is no longer
than a day. It is the child
within a child you cry for.
She sits upright between pillows,
her dark hair tied back
with pink ribbons.
She is between sheets
that smell of soap and sun
and all the games of summer.
She knows the shadows posts make,
that wind pulls her curtains out,
pushes them in again. All crickets
sing to her. You want that now.

By the bed is a round red rug,
slippery on the wax glossed floor.
A doll lamp plays and spins
to the gold key in her back,
a stuffed dog has lost its ear.
You want that child
who believes everything will always
be all right and her mother and father
sleep across the hall. There are milk
and cake in the kitchen . . . your favorite
kind. On the shelf is the shepherdess
figurine, a Christmas plate of three
angels. It is Easter now and the world
bright as eggs, but the Old Troll
under the bridge has collected. You can't
go back. Morning is silver. The next
troll under the next bridge knows
what he wants. He has your name.
You know his.

Housecleaning

Clean was what we wanted.
Clean as moonlight, clean
as grass after rain, clean as
fish or feet running in new dew.
We wanted to do in one day
what God did only better,
chasing devils out
with magic brooms, doing
away with evils seen
and hidden. Later,
we would know the meaning
and costs, but then was only
starched days, air of soap
and something sun gives
gradually ebbing back,
over and under while you sleep
or stand to see, but never quite.

With buckets and brushes,
we washed winter off
under clouds hung
like sails. Curtains
hooked on nails no one could
or would walk for truth
or faith or any clean reason.
Clean, was what we wanted.

Bedsprings were hauled to sawhorses
and hosed. Mattresses aired
from the shape of sleep, stirred
from dust, bed kittens rousted out.
Whatever couldn't be scrubbed

was shook and sunned. Screens,
when brushed, sang. We washed sills,
whooshed wasps and spiders out,
cinders and soot, out, out.
We were elves in the service
of something next to God.

Newspapers lined shelves so we could
See in a year where the day had been.
In the afternoon, netted squares
of gauze, stiff as wafers, stood
alone and tall. Ruffled edges
with picot rim, prickled holes
in the night, let pinpoints
of day strain through.

Red zinnias in a vase on an oiled table
stood in a gleaming world
of one small space.

Leaf Raking Poem
Every poet has one.
—Dave Smith

I grew up without trees.
At three I knew only a post oak
that never shed; tall and splayed
offered me roots, pretend alligators,
horses, trains. I went nowhere
I couldn't get home again.
Not water, nor flood, nor my father's
hard cursing ghost at the blue wheel
making ways where there were none.
Across gravel, low water bridges, I heard
her say, "Wild horses couldn't keep you
from what you'd do." And he said back,
"Dammit, ruin your life like I ruined
mine."

The pale bedroom I had at seven
wore curtains ballooning in and out;
green trees, water, pastures. I'd cried
for those curtains, knew even in a stifling
city, I'd have trees, a place to climb
in my mind. Not the usual symbol,
but life as it branches and leafed
in my lungs.

At twelve there was a party where games
became a hill of leaves. We rolled in them,
thighs tickled by boys who chased
then sat astride, wrestling, flinging leaves.
Joy sang in my veins in being
a girl whose body worked for no one but her.

Spring and fall, I'd borrow a neighbor's
maples, tall candles out my window.

In April, I blew winged planes
from fingertips like green dragonflies.
I'd wrestle, holding wings between my fingers.
No one came but the self
I'd shoved aside like a sibling.
Those leaves like hands, stars,
tulips cut in half, raked with my feet, kicking the
chill winds away.
October leaves above a creek
made a cinnamon sea for sleep.
You said sun streamed ribbons
in my hair, across your chest.
A clacking creek warned us of years,
my seventeen, your forty-three.
We snapped twigs off a tree
whose leaves I kept pressed
in pages, 50 red, few and mine.

We stole leaves.
Great robbery bags of them,
shoved like passengers on a tour boat,
lifted from streetcorners.
They went willingly, eager, hot and damp.
We unloaded them at midnight for mulch,
all for the grounds good
and some groceries.

Later, I lived in a land owned
by oaks, sweetgum, sassafras, shagbark
hickories, mulberry, cedars, a few fine
pines, ironwood and willow.
Never raked. I watched winters
whirl and lift leaves
spin like a glass paperweight
world reversed. I watched
five winters, then walked
and never thought back.

Yes

A word that opens its mouth
and closes its eyes.
I wonder who said it first,
and whether for love
or hunger.

Dowry

Mother seamed my legs together,
said run but don't step on the grass.
She made me a cap of bridal lace,
fitted it with wire. This will
keep you warm, she said, and your
thinking straight. She taught me
to count to 28 and back, to depend
on the moon, chart tides, make my face
a clock. Showed me how to pour tea,
service always with a smile. She folded
my arms to hold babies and brooms.
Put pebbles in my mouth and said swallow.
She coaxed my voice to sing all the notes
of content. At her elbow, she taught
me the ways of fire, its principal use
to keep a man home. She never showed me
how to count coins, nor fitted my shoulder
for a gun. She didn't tell me the words
to save my life. Instead, I was made
to whisper quiet mumblings
to a white fur muff.

Mother,
today making my bed, I found the pea.
It was under the mattress seventh
from the floor. I knew from the first
and would have cried each night
except for numbness and the fact
that for years I have knotted sheets
of lasting escape.

Making the Bed

*Unhappiness may be only a mistake.
A mental mistake, that you could
still undo.*
—Margaret Fuller

Staying Over

Turn out the lights.
It is only ghost stories,
yours, mine, whoever appears
soundless or still shouting.
We never find that space between us
filled and whole, but wedged
as dawn. What warms us
is neither love, nor anger,
but something older,
full of light and green as dreams.
We count the times a whippoorwill
calls in an hour, owls at three a.m.,
cat in our window rubbing
the screen in a whisper
while the moon sits somewhere
looking and listening.

Making the Bed

No matter how well
or worse the sleep
someone must take
the four cornered world
and set it straight.
Two can do it better,
take turns with edges,
coverlet, shams,
blanket and bolster,
wait in turn.

You can do it in the dark,
by feel, familiarity,
plumping feathers or foam.
You know your own scent,
shallow spots your knees
seek, the place you
fall into, dark and faraway,
taking you back or forward
like a train, all scenes
lighted cars you can look into,
out again. You hear the engine
that goes nowhere, the solitary
shriek as daybreak unrolls,
all wrappings out like flowers.

We go on with our lives.

Laundry

All our life
so much laundry;
each day's doing or not
comes clean,
flows off and away
to blend with other sins
of this world. Each day
begins in new skin,
blessed by the elements
charged to take us
out again to do or undo
what's been assigned.
From socks to shirts
the selves we shed
lift off the line
as if they own
a life apart
from the one we offer.
There is joy in clean laundry.
All is forgiven in water, sun
and air. We offer our day's deeds
to the blue-eyed sky, with soap and prayer,
our arms up, then lowered in supplication.

Another Name

Marriage, she said,
should have another name.
Roses wreathed her hair,
ivy over each ear.
She whispered between
cake and ferns,
glass gifts,
leftover children
mumbled about the room.
The moon
sat on her head,
nodded, but didn't
give the other word.
Laughter took off her shoes
and danced, the rugs rolled
back, bare floors polished
and kind. Sorrow
took the arm of tears
and did a slow waltz
into the night quiet
as sin. Cello spun
his bass around
and the harp stood
on someone's toes.
A good party,
this wedding.
We know the other
name.

Marriage Portions

The room of a room is smaller
than those we fought in: you pacing,
me in the blue chair beside lamps
each wanted. But it wasn't always so.
Early we divided walls and floors
in half; your albums, my books,
the chair your mother gave us, I gave
back. Screamed into the face
of my father's father's clock,
refused to let go. It stopped,
pendulum mute as a severed tongue.
There was the rug you couldn't roll
when I stood center and said
I'd take scissors, saw, some serrated
knife before I'd let you leave
with the land of my lunch hours
I'd spent sales hungrily hunting.

The rest was easy
until we came to the crib.
I said mine, mine, but he wasn't
and isn't. Neither owned him.
Now we have other furniture,
rooms like a marriage museum
and the son takes a life
on longer than we thought
in that room of a room.

Safe Houses

In that little Fifties box,
tacked to the hillside,
row matching row, she felt safe;
good girl, all As, wax protected,
soapy clean. There wallpaper bloomed,
plants grew . . . one bean vine covered a wall.
They made a patio, wove a privacy fence,
grilled out every summer Saturday.
She had a rose trellis,
like the song said, and every Easter,
iris wept lavender, washing blue
over her fingertips and down, portents
of terror inside.
They almost took him; the first son,
she birthed twice and sometimes
seven times a night
until he was twelve. Then her husband
took over, told him things she never knew.
Scare stories of boys in the world
where bears were behind every bush,
lions lay on every limb.

o, their lives then,
in picture window castles,
each bedroom a pipeline fueling
the need to know, repeat, exchange.
Someone always peeped.
Someone always listened.
Entertainment was the cheapest thing
all week with few questions kept
longer than a wink.

That grid never fitted, but
she moved in pretense, made herself
a suit of mail that clanked
louder each step she walked.

The moat didn't stop her, though
he paved it with money and the soil
on the other side smelled sweeter
than the first air she breathed.

Findings

A pink button in the back
of the bottom drawer; rabbit's eye
reflecting light, the past, and a jacket
I wore twenty years ago. Loopy nubs,
round velvet collar, loosely fitted;
I fitted inside and inside me, our son.
He grew until the coat no longer
buttoned us together, except in a photograph
I remember. There I stood in the corner
of the picture of our first house,
white with green shutters, a window box
I planted ivy, forgot to water. Its dried
strings hang from the sides like fingers.
The camera caught my swollen girlhood
full profile. You said you were photographing
the house and I was not in range. o Love,
you thought me beautiful, bursting from that pink
coat shell, which the son has now long shed
and I, somehow, have kept the button.

Tin Years

It wasn't her fault, he came home
from the office at 10 AM,
stayed twelve years?
The house where Washington
Road met Cornwallis Lane was cut
in half by pride. Ashes
on that fixed mortgage hearth
collected like cinders and the brass
knocker on the colonial blue door
tarnished green. Ivy
couldn't hide
the fact he quit, ran to sit
in the corner like Cinderella
waited for work to find him.
Lord, it was hard
keeping the kids in shoes,
herself in skirts going store
to store, trying to sell herself
in never the package she meant to present.
Tough juggler of magic,
she tugged silver from her sleeves,
behind her head, out her ear.
He never noticed.
She can tell you
about the second ten years;
after the bliss.
You learn to forgive.
Yourself first. After the gown
of guilt gets haircloth coarse.
Those years
of no money, no plans
where time wore everything
they owned.

On Her Way to Meet Her Lover, She Forgives Her Father

Coming and going
the same lonely woman
at the wheel
on a road where only seasons change.
The light goes day to dark
to day again. She goes and the going is rote;
this dark-eyed stranger
driving hell-bent for somewhere
fast. Track the lives
and those wheels rolling
like rivers while the sky melts
into curtains of something
confining her to the car
moving up mountains,
moving up mornings, the long
alleys of evening.

This is the woman
finding her father when she parks
a pencil behind her ear.
He wore his there
writing tickets in a numbered
pad, his careless scrawl
lives in her life of excuses,
little blames she tried to lay
at his grave. Driving,
she knows now, what he did
outside his job only
meant pleasure, not harm
though it hurt her
sixteenth year, and twenty, thirty.
By forty she was beginning

to understand ten hour
days owned by an omniscient
god of the payroll voucher
can drain your life
in so many directions,
that asking won't give anything
guaranteed. Not this whirling
world nor the next.

Each day she begins in one direction,
follows as far as the contract
that keeps her going.
Paper words pull her
from the forest of sleep
where bears held her thoughts
like a winter life
and owls waked her hunting.

Hunting, her father
never a crack shot
bagged only small game,
brought it home bloody
warm and limp in his pockets.
Unfastened the snaps
he palmed the featherbed,
furred creatures out
like alms. She wanted
none of it except their lives
back, cried while
he called it only a game.
Making things twice
worse and she couldn't tell him
in her eyes he stood
only two feet tall.
Giant father on the horse
riding hell-bent

to hell, the husbands
sending him out with fists.

She thinks of pain,
how we never know,
truly know, another's
depth, nor the stepping
in their skin. Till she meets
herself, this strange woman
is not her sister, daughter,
but someone who has worn the same
clothes, friends, memory scars,
knows the road and takes the wheel
whether she wants it or not.

Father, Son and Oranges

1.
At the end of a January
I stand over my kitchen sink
peeling holiday oranges,
hard rinds of tight juices.
I think of my father who
carried home sacks
of shining fruit, gold
in the mesh gray arm of winter.
His hands large as he turned
his mouth a Chinese lantern,
spilling peel around him like petals,
cardboard puzzle, a soft world
unwound. Crystal strings
of juices curled the fingers
bees tasted. Keeper of the hive,
jack-in-the-box of buzzing music
rich as honey, strained sun,
ripe and sealed warm in a jar.

2.
My son brings oranges.
Exchanged his check for gold,
he walks tired as a miner,
his eyes burnt lamps
When my father was ill and dying,
he wanted oranges, said they didn't
taste like he remembered. When my son
was ill, he wanted oranges, said
they burned his mouth. He peels
them like a potter, stacks the shells,
emptied as eggs.

3.
Once, stranded on a train
in Orange, Virginia, at 2 AM
I ate two pears left from my lunch
in that overheated box of bodies.
We sat like a scene from *Dr. Zhivago*.
The train rocked back, back
into the night and our orange
window spread sections of light
onto the covered ground.
My husband slept, one eye
awake on a booted blond, furs
to her chin. I peeled pears
alone and cold in the snow
in Orange, Virginia. My father
is dead. My son has chosen
over me and I can only peel
hard oranges, forgotten
as promises. The juice spills
over my hands, a melting dessert;
kisses from a child, I gave my father,
my son gave me and the husband
eats Ambrosia
        late at night
        alone with his letters.

Bagpipes

I.
In the tent they waited
for haggis; forks paused,
plates warm,
glasses filled for toasting.
The piper came first.
In plaid and tassels
he played the story with pipes
and flourishes, marched through,
then back again.
Her husband held his ears,
got under a chair
where he stuck like gum.
She feared he'd sit
on his haunches and howl.
Instead he stayed until
the haggis was eaten, toasts
given and everyone gone.

II.
In a motel in Media, PA,
travel tired and nearing sleep,
she heard bagpipes.
Through double walls
and insulated windows,
they wound around her day
and found her.
She went to the balcony.
Below was a full regalia
of every plaid possible, kilts
and tams, bagpipes charming the summer air.
They practiced an hour, marched

to the festival on her applause.
Her husband stayed inside,
heard only the tv news.

III.
On a lonely Saturday night
their notes floated over a high fence
and came for her. She followed
a piper, lonely as sound.
He played for himself, the fields,
Robert, an Irish Setter,
and her, though he didn't know
she heard.

They went from
pipes to Scotch
to stories
to comforters
to bed
while her husband slept
beyond, over and across the ridge.
He knew she wasn't dreaming
at all.

Dialogue: Mother to Son
(Apology for Receding Hair)

At twenty-five your father had as much
as any male, more of other things.
Intellect, I think, attracted me.
Ambition. I didn't see an abundance,
but ideas? He swam
with them. Not a jock,
you'll have to forgive me.
Sports,
even as a spectator
have never held me.
We battled wits,
lived on them for thirty years.
When I could laugh no longer,
I called it off.
But that was a long time after
the work went out.

You didn't shave
until you were seventeen
and then only once a week
because you wanted the feel
of cool metal
cutting the surface
where a crop
could sprout.

Absence of chest hair?
Facial? Again, apology.
I truly never noticed.
All I can give you,
son, is a toupee of blessings,
the birthright you can cheat for,
your brother's dark curse.

Think how I held him
a month from the lion's jaws.
There you were,
bald at two,
onion bright and not even enough on the nape
to curl.

Look, where hair has gotten
history. Sampson? Baldness
might have saved him, the rest
of us. Think where Rapunzel's lover fell.
Sir Gwain's green friend?
Belinda's lock?

Oh son, don't steal, buy or borrow,
covet. That won't cover a thing.
The world looks at twenty,
as false as forty.

I give you gumption
to know hair isn't all it's owned
to be, can be bought or sold.
Dark suits thank you,
drains as well.

Sunday in the Park with God and Sparrows

A sparrow drinks
from the dripping faucet
in the marigolds garden;
their ginger scent sharp
as the hawk hovering
on the live oak limb
From the Episcopal Church
muted songs, careful prayers
even sparrows pray. You deny.
"Nietzsche was right," you say,
"Three hundred in a church,
three hundred gods."

I think of the story you tell
of your baptismal day.
How you hid under stairs.
Then it thundered, lightened
and finally they found you
crouched as pigeons crouch
below the hawk. I am like
the sparrows shrieking,
"Thereheis, thereheis."

You denied, became instead
king for an hour
as many hours as you own.
God isn't the hawk,
nor sparrow, nor Nietzsche
in church. Believe me.
God is a marigold.

Sleep

*One can't think about death steadily
any more than one can stare at the sun.
I think about it slant.*
— Emily Dickinson

Penelope, After

That bed.
He carved it like a totem,
every mark a meaning,
every nick with his knife
more than symbol. For me
he carved roses.
For himself, laughing,
he carved ivy and figs.
I lay remembering his red beard
like fire on my breasts.

I was the weaving wren, my nest
unwound each day like light.
Those tortoise years
I painted myself more pious
than a nun. But it was more
than a matter of waiting, though
I did both well, tending threads,
his father, son, houses and farms,
holding firm in the middle. Forever
was the rusty bolt in my life.
Faithful was twenty years
too long. My wall
hung with weavings, seeing
what I'd said with my days,
I dismissed those maids,
Solitude and Fidelity.
He had more
than a hero's chance at war, but
some have to cross the last wall,
look back, to see what they had.

George Eliot: Letter to John Cross

The canal, dear, of all places.
Softer than streets of course,
but it's a wonder you survived
the water.

Before you jumped from the balcony,
you mentioned a headache.
Both of us knew it was more
than a honeymoon hangover,
more than bedcovers
could contain
or keep hidden.

I'll never believe it was lack
of exercise or bad air.
Dante did us in.
Dante, Dante.
We read Paolo and Francesca
forgot where we were.
Spirit runs the body
only so far,
then age takes over.

That ferryman boats
every river in the world
choked with guilt.

He Licked Wine From My Fingers
(The Death of Robert Schumann)

July 29, 1856 Endenich
Bonn, Germany

From Clara's Diary:

For two years and more
the doctors have kept me
from Robert, saying they feared
a complete relapse. Even my letters
they forbade. I relied on reports
from dear friends, tormenting myself
he was better. I had to look after myself
and the children. Truly I believed
someday he would be restored
to his work, his family.
The day he was taken away
I felt my heart had been ripped
from me. He left in a fever
cloaked in despair.

Now, in his last hours,
they let me in
and I hardly knew the husband
I had, the Robert I loved.
Everything around him seemed holy;
the light on his face
came from within, his wonderful hands
glowed like marble; hands that had pulled
music
from air, the deepest part
of his being. I know he knew me.
Somehow in his fever of words
I heard "Clara, my Clara."

For weeks, they said,
he'd taken nothing
but calves's foot jelly
and a little wine.
I know he knew me.
He licked wine from my fingers.

At four thirty this afternoon
his terrible agony ended.
He left us. What sorrow.
What desolation.

River Bed

You make your bed
by the river where willows
dip and smooth the flowing.
Stars beneath swallowed
by fish and somewhere
on the sweet ground, you sleep;
a blanket of oaks
shut out the sky.

When you wake late
you find cobblestones,
brown as a ditch.
The river, gone
for the power of one
hand on the switch
where Monday's mill
will spin the cotton
into sheets, spin
the cotton into sheets.

You believed in rivers—
that what was going
would go on past fall
rising and summer drought.
You thought you could
put your hand in, pull it back
and see where you had been.
You knew sunlight on water
never really touched anything
but your own sight. Still,
you made your bed
out from under

and walked
willow to willow, pretending
there was water,
and the sound did not stop
whether you heard or not.

You came from that lake
wearing cattails, thoughts
like scales. Guilty, guilty,
you made your bed wanting stories
where all ends well—not wisely,
just well.

And the cradle in the attic
stayed full of old newspapers.

You made your bed
on the pine, under a tin roof,
in the rain. You rarely
think for the roar,
think for the roar.

Blackberry Wine

The bed she died in
my grandfather never knew.
Summers she slept
in the front bedroom; white walled
and honeysuckle scented lace
curtains fingered by wind
from three tall windows.
She slept on feather pillows
plucked and filled by no hands
but hers.

That August, that
dry, dry August, she spent
in the place between dark and day,
sipping soup, cool tea, honey water,
cracked ice and finally nothing
but blackberry wine. This teetotaler
who'd never touched whiskey nor
soda, drank her wine, told a risque
joke and laughed; this quiet woman
of the pious face, Victorian ways.
Grandmother told of an old maid,
a nun, and the man who came
in the night.

Death listened
found she was not afraid, took her hand.
At ninety-three she knew
she couldn't outbluff him,
so she went
calling her greeting ahead.

Double Bed

After she died
he took her bed
that place denied
those many years,
bed with pineapple posts,
double wedding ring quilt.
He moved her vanity
so the oval mirror
couldn't see
his eighty years nakedness.
Each night
he pulls the string
to out the light, enters
her shape, soft and curved
as flesh.

My Grandfather's Bed

My grandfather's bed
stood a thousand pillows high
and he was made of wax,
his hands limp and white
on the sheet of snow.
His breath came slow and close
while his eyes of stone lay
round as marbles.
The ceiling fell fast upon him
but couldn't hold him down.
Out the window he went
in his air night gown
bare-boned legs
leaping like something dark ran after.
His last horse was the wind
back when we least expected him
never forgetting the least
of our sins nor grabbling
after his ghost.

Afternoon of a Father-in-Law

My father-in-laws slippers
knock overhead.
Not an elderly shuffle
with his slippers but a sharp
knock, knocking of impatient heels
pacing. And walking I hear
how he sounded
in halls as his own wife died.
He walked watching his shoes
dot dark with tears.
And after, in the silence,
lit lamps in the attic,
blazed a trail to the barn
where the cows of his childhood
milled and chewed.

His mother. Always mama s boy,
lost lamb on the rack
of a failing farm.
The son not one he wanted;
a musician, an artist who left
for school the first opening
in the city.
And the daughter brought
home a fun filled fellow who laughed
at anything akin to work, but
ving, ving, ving grandchildren
popped like peas.

His wife
ripped her heart in half
and handed it to them
wrapped in foil. They

gave it back, stuffed
with shredded cheese.
Knocking, knocking, his walk
down the hospital walls
to bed and back where
he won't sleep,
can't close his door
for fear who's there.

Restless
his knocking
until someone answers.

Crocheted

How she holds our lives:
missing mother, veiled madonna,
shrouded saint. Around the table
we line up like chairs.
Her tablecloth, roses and briars,
says she was here. Her hands
knotted, pulled cat's cradles
in the air, in our hair,
behind our necks.

Yes, she fed us
and we ate. Little lies
like sweet meringues,
Baked Alaska Pie
of the past, o we partook.
Knowing all love was like this,
each family shared
smoke from the kitchen,
burnt bitterness acid as grapes
she brined to vinegar
poured in our wounds.

Then her daughter in the attic
fought, claimed for herself only
sweaters and scarves made in Japan.
Not what the mother fingers
wove bleeding with cuts and thorns.

Her needle hooked our lives.
She chained blood
and sewed our bones
tight to the sack of her side.

Packhorse, packrat mother,
pull the cord and rise.

Flannel Pajamas

*I always had a theory that if a thing
served its purpose well it would be
beautiful.*
—Carl Sandburg

You never had a fabric in your life
worthy of your fingers. You made
leftovers, castoffs, bargains better.
Stitched each seam twice and straight.
I marvel at your craft
on something so nightly,
utility, this poor man's warmth.
Pajama's Eve would have made Adam
if she'd owned a needle.
And flannel. Pajamas
your son felt were his Christmas curse.
Pajamas and underwear, baggy boxers
you made from brown diamonds, green
squares he swore left everything
loose, falling out. He rebelled
to jockey, sleeping nude.
Your gift pajamas under the pillow
in case of cold or flu.

Five years after you died
your husband's heart squeezed,
burned. In intensive care,
he wore nothing but tubes, monitors,
a single sheet. I took him pajamas
you made, washed, line-dried, soft
with your stitching. I see you now
steady as the treadle under
your foot, under the lamp, you gliding
flannel like a landscape
over hills, down valleys,
then into a human shape.

Sleep

> *We are but older children, dear,*
> *Who fret to find our bedtime near.*
> —Lewis Carroll

Only we in the middle
fool themselves, finding respite
in dark hours of knitted numbness.
Babies, too close to that first dark
when everything
curled in total care,
fear what they can't name.
The rope of it pulls them
like a divers signal,
keeps them home,
alert, even if exploring
new air. The length grows
and they dance farther
and faster until no line
is left. Watch them as they run.

Those on the other end
know sleep as thief, who takes
scraps and threads
of all they own. Making off with
their lives hour by hour.
Until the last one. That sneak
lingers and laughs as he leads
the way to the longest nap.

Single Bed

We come to it;
narrowing our lives
to fit the lone bed
where we pillow our head,
fit our feet
at the foot
measuring ourselves
out. There are those
over us. Those
under us
and the middle
where the music is.
Memory sits
atop one bedpost;
your mother
the other.
Your father scolds
from the bureau drawer
and the ghost of your girlhood
sits on the closet shelf,
swinging her small
white
feet.

A Note About the Author

Ruth Moose is the author of two short story collections: *The Wreath Ribbon Quilt* (St. Andrews Press) and *Dreaming in Color* (August House). She has had stories published in *The Atlantic Monthly*, *Ohio Review*, *New Delta Review* and three stories in *Redbook*. She has published four collections of poetry, *To Survive* (Bookmark Press), *Finding Things in the Dark* (Briarpatch Press), *Making the Bed* (Sandstone Press/Pure Heart Press) and *Smith Grove*, illustrated by Talmadge Moose (Sow's Ear Press.) She edited *12 Christmas Stories by NC Writers*, illustrated by Talmadge Moose (DownHome Press) and *I Have Walked, A Collection of Stories and Poem on Poverty* (NC Humanities).

She has received a North Carolina Writers Fellowship, Three Pen Awards for syndicated fiction, Yankee Magazine Awards for poetry, the Carl Sandburg Award, the Oscar Arnold Young Award and a McDowell Fellowship.

Ruth Moose has been on the faculty of the Creative Writing Department at the University of North Carolina since 1996.